Trollheimen

A Solo Female Wanderer Hiking Guide

Introduction

Trollheimen is one of the best destinations for hiking in Norway. The terrain goes from alpine peaks to agricultural valleys, and the routes stay in serviced cabins and luxurious self-service cabins. There are loops from three days to ten days and plenty of options for every hiking level.

It's also easy to get to on the train or bus from Trondheim, so it's easy to add onto a trip to Norway.

Table of Contents

Route Combinations

Wondering where to get started? Here are four possible cabin to cabin itineraries in Trollheimen:

Classic Trollheimen Triangle

The classic three day hike. The days are long but not technically challenging, and it's one of the best starter cabin to cabin hikes in Norway. I met everyone from families to dedicated mountaineers to retirees when I did it. If you're looking for a first cabin to cabin hike, or a good long weekend getaway, I recommend it.

Route	Page	Length (km)	Elevation Gain (m)	Elevation Drop (m)	Time (ut. no)
Gjevilvasshytta to Jøldalshytta	10	17.0	581	248	6
Jøldalshytta to Trollheimshytta via Geithetta	12	16.5	678	884	6
Trollheimshytta to Gjevilvasshytta	28	21.1	1,027	853	8

West Trollheimen Triangle

Three to four days of hiking in the less visited and more alpine side of the park. The terrain is slightly more challenging than the Trollheimen Triangle classic route. To reach this via public transportation, add two days to hike in and out from Eiriksvollen.

Route	Page	Length (km)	Elevation Gain (m)	Elevation Drop (m)	Time (ut.no)
Innerdalen to Bårdsgarden via Langvatnet	20	23.7	897	670	8
Bårdsgarden to Kårvatn	36	22.0	486	891	6
Kårvatn to Innerdalen	18	13.0	978	781	5

Trollheimen SignaTUR

A seven day hike that hits most of the major attractions in Trollheimen, staying in a mixture of serviced and self-service cabins. DNT's SignaTUR hikes are long hikes covering a variety of landscapes.

Route	Page	Length (km)	Elevation Gain (m)	Elevation Drop (m)	Time (ut. no)
Gjevilvasshytta to Jøldalshytta	10	17.0	581	248	6
Jøldalshytta to Trollheimshytta via Geithetta	12	16.5	678	884	6
Trollheimshytta to Kårvatn	16	23.0	559	886	8
Kårvatn to Innerdalen	18	13.0	978	781	5
Innerdalen to Bårdsgarden via Langvatnet	20	23.7	897	670	8
Bårdsgarden to Vassendsetra	22	18.9	966	921	5
Vassendsetra to Gjevilvasshytta via Riaren	24	22.1	1,005	994	7

Ten-ish Days in Trollheimen

This route combines the Trollheimen SignaTUR with the Trollheimen Triangle. Start by doing the four days below, then complete the Trollheimen SignaTUR.

Route	Page	Length (km)	Elevation Gain (m)	Elevation Drop (m)	Time (ut. no)
Sætersetra and Vindølbu	30	12.1	958	545	4.5
Vindølbu to Trollheimshytta	32	19.1	736	682	6
Day trip to Snota	14	23.4	1,337	1,337	9
Trollheimshytta to Gjevilvasshytta	28	21.1	1,027	853	8

Hike Overview

Route	Page	Ending cabin
From Gjevilvasshytta to Jøldalshytta	10	Jøldalshytta
From Jøldalshytta to Trollheimshytta via Geithetta	12	Trollheimshytta
From Jøldalshytta to Trollheimshytta via Svartådalen	12	Trollheimshytta
From Jøldalshytta to Trollheimshytta via summits	12	Trollheimshytta
Day trip to Snota	14	Trollheimshytta
From Trollheimshytta to Kårvatn	16	Kårvatn
From Kårvatn to Innerdalen	18	Innerdalshytta
From Innerdalen to Bårdsgarden via Langvatnet	20	Bårdsgarden
From Innerdalen to Bårdsgarden via Innerdalsporten	20	Bårdsgarden
From Bårdsgarden to Vassendsetra over Okla	22	Vassendsetra
From Vassendsetra to Gjevilvasshytta via lake	24	Gjevilvasshytta
From Vassendsetra to Gjevilvasshytta via Riaren	24	Gjevilvasshytta
Day trip to Blåhøa	26	Gjevilvasshytta
Trollheimshytta to Gjevilvasshytta	28	Gjevilvasshytta
Sætersetra and Vindølbu from Øvre Sæter	30	Vindølbu
From Vindølbu to Trollheimshytta	32	Trollheimshytta
Innerdalshytta to Eiriksvollen	34	Eiriksvollen
Bårdsgarden to Kårvatn	36	Kårvatn

Trollheimen's hikes are long - it's quite difficult to combine cabins and do two segments in a single day.

Length (km)	Elevation Gain (m)	Elevation Drop (m)	Time (ut.no)
17.0	581	248	6
16.5	678	884	6
16.0	125	331	5
19.9	1,159	1,365	9
23.4	1,337	1,337	9
23.0	559	886	8
13.0	978	781	5
23.7	897	670	8
22.1	707	480	7
18.9	966	921	6
12.9	194	183	3.5
22.1	1,005	994	7
25.0	1,193	1,193	6
21.1	1,027	853	8
12.1	958	545	4.5
19.1	736	682	6
14.3	646	958	6
22.0	486	891	7

UT.no gives the times for an average Norwegian hiker with a backpack. Your times will vary.

Gjevilvasshytta to Jøldalshytta

17.0 km
10.6 miles

581 meters
1,906 feet

248 meters
814 feet

6 hours
Challenging

This is a relatively long but technically easy hike. The trail starts by going up a farm road behind Gjevilvasshytta, through a farm with sheep and goats. The trail turns to dirt and continues through a forest, gently climbing the whole way. Eventually, the trail passes out of the forest and gets into open mountain terrain, with views on the mountains in the distance on either side. The path is easy to follow through this section and relatively flat. The drop to Jøldalshytta is on dirt, and then there's a short section on farm roads again - it's technically very easy, but watch out for gifts from the sheep and goats nearby.

My notes

This is a long hike, but the terrain isn't too challenging - lots of views, lots of wilderness, and no rock scrambling. Despite the number of people at both cabins, I never felt like the trail was crowded - in fact, I went most of the day without seeing anyone.

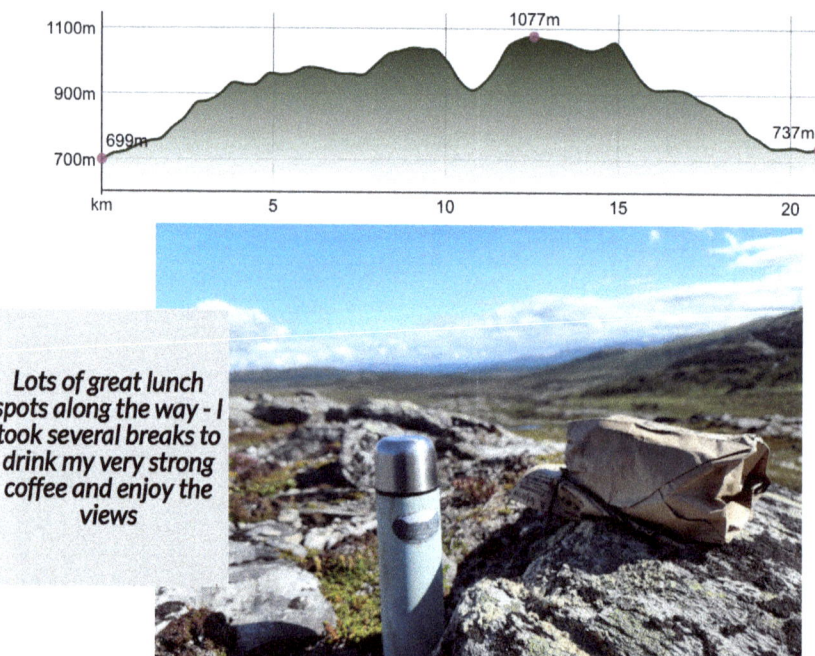

Lots of great lunch spots along the way - I took several breaks to drink my very strong coffee and enjoy the views

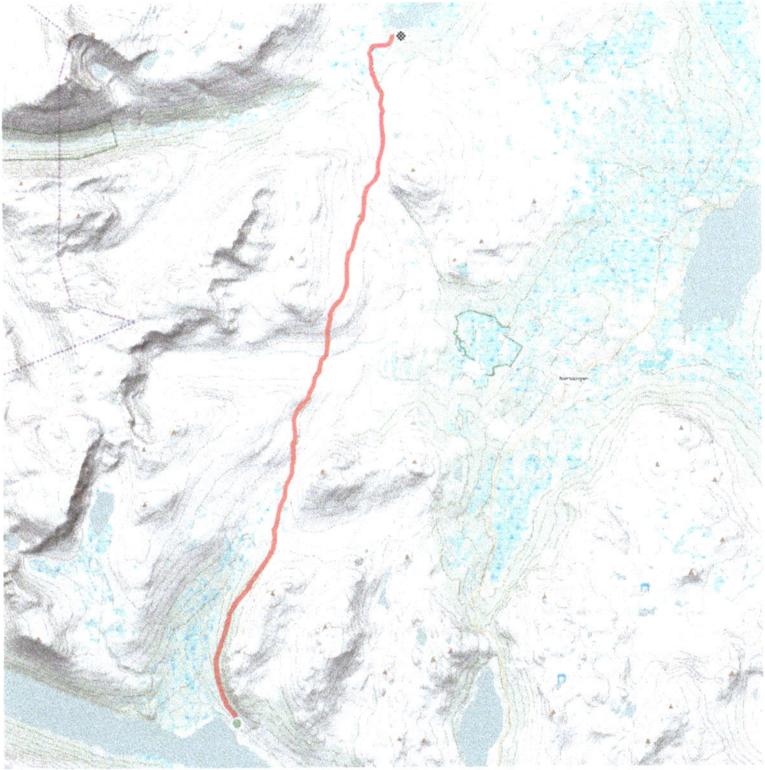

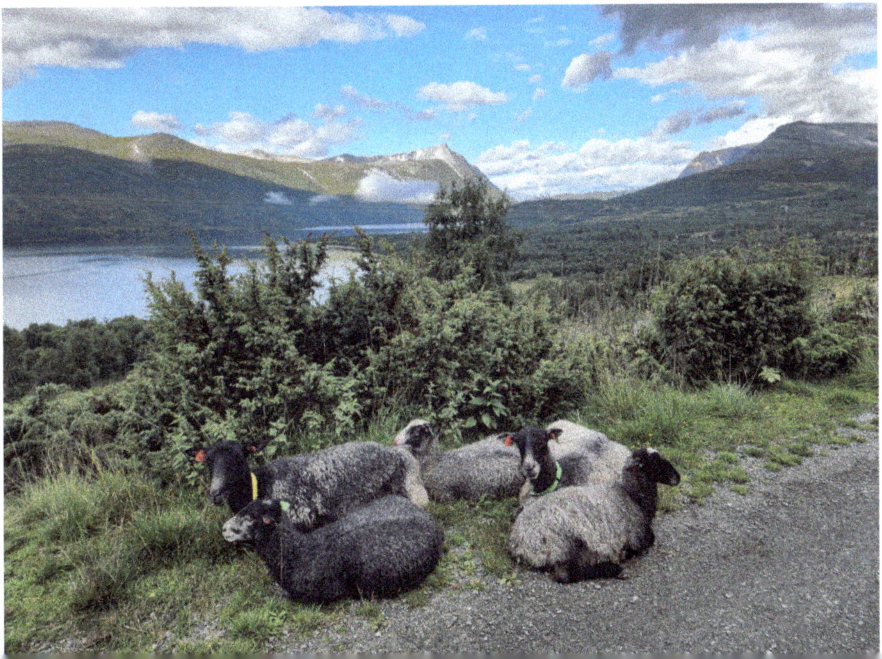

Jøldalshytta to Trollheimshytta

	👢	↗	↘	🕐
Svartådalen	16.0 km 9.9 miles	125 meters 410 feet	331 meters 1,086 feet	5 hours Moderate
Geithetta	16.5 km 10.3 miles	678 meters 2,224 feet	884 meters 2,900 feet	6 hours Challenging
Summits	19.9 km 12.4 miles	1,159 meters 3,802 feet	1,365 meters 4,478 feet	9 hours Very challenging

There are three separate routes that you can take from Jøldalshytta to Trollheimshytta:

Marked paths over Geithetta. Start by going along the route through the Svartådalen for 6 kilometers. This section is mainly on dirt roads and wide, flat trails. After that, the trail to Geithetta branches off from the Svartådalen trail to the south. The trail climbs gradually up to the Geithetta ridge - not to the summit, which is not marked. After going along the ridge, the trail drops very steeply down next to a waterfall and then goes 1.5 kilometers through a potentially swampy section until it reaches Trollheimshytta.

Over three summits of Trollhetta. This is a difficult route, especially if the weather isn't cooperating. Start by going a kilometer on the trail heading west from Jøldalshytta, then turn towards the right/north and follow the cairns to start climbing steeply up Langfjellet. From here, the trail flattens out for a bit, following the ridge on Langfjellet, then climbs again to go up to the eastern summit of Trollhøtta at eleven to twelve kilometers of total hiking. After this, there's a section that has a very steep drop off to the side, so go slowly and be careful. There can be loose rock in this section, and it's particularly difficult if it's raining. The terrain on the descent is initially rocky, followed by myr and then a fir forest. Meet up with the trail coming from Rindal and then turn towards the south to reach Trollheimshytta, 1-2 kilometers after the intersection.

Down through the Svartådalen The trail goes west from Jøldalshytta and then continues through the valley alongside the river for fifteen kilometers. There are sections that can be wet, especially if it's rained recently, but the terrain is easy to hike along. With about a kilometer left, the trail turns towards the southwest and goes to Trollheimshytta, leaving the river.

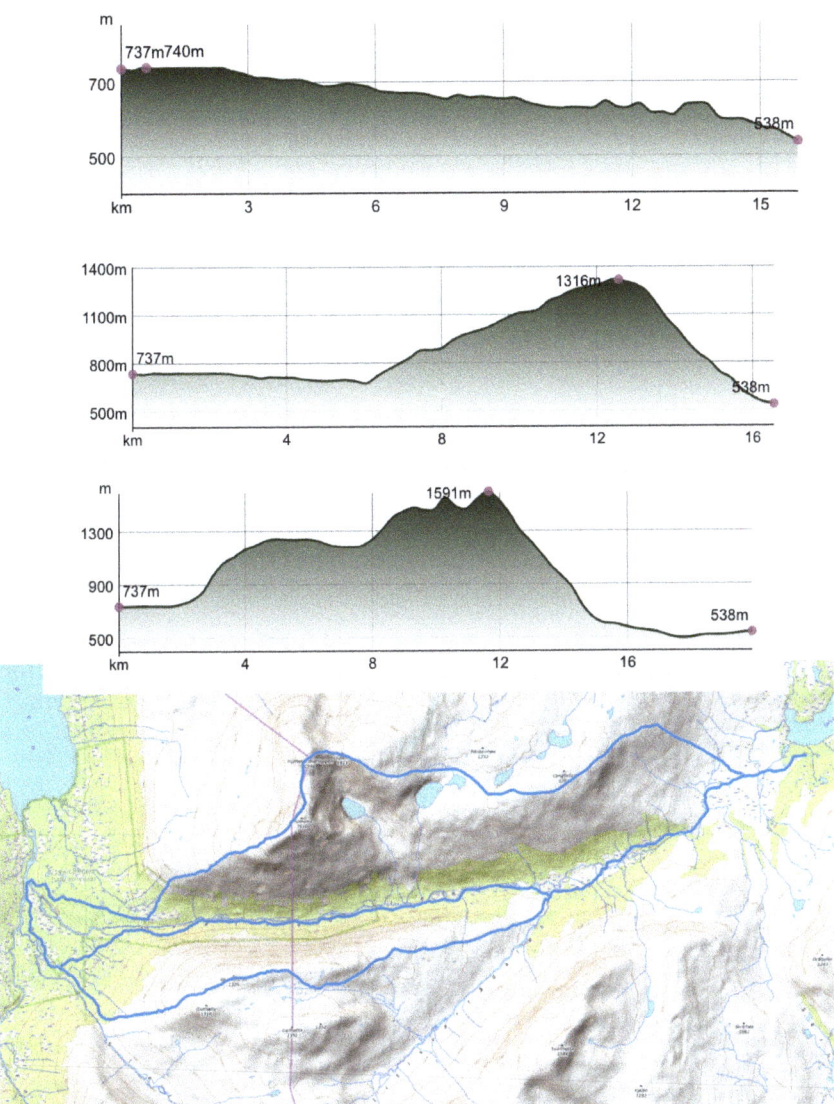

My notes:

Geithetta had fantastic views without the terrain being too challenging, while the route through the valley was flat and a good way to rest your legs if they're tired from the days before.

Trollheimshytta doesn't have phone service, so check the weather and send messages before you get there. (But they serve an extra dessert after dinner, which makes up for the lack of phone service.)

Snota from Trollheimshytta

| 23.4 km | 1,337 meters | 1,337 meters | 9 hours |
| 14.5 miles | 4,386 feet | 4,386 feet | Very challenging |

Snota is the iconic Trollheimen peak, and it's a popular day trip destination from Trollheimshytta. This is a challenging hike, especially if there's strong rain or wind.

The trail starts from Trollheimshytta, following signs towards Vindølbu and Snota. The trail passes over a bridge over the river Slettåa and then one over the river Folda. About 300 meters after the second bridge, the trail starts to climb up through a birch forest, then enters a valley with quite a bit of myr, a bog-like ground covering. The trail is relatively flat through this section. Myr can be difficult to hike through if it's rained recently.

After about five kilometers of hiking, the trail reaches an intersection. At the intersection, take the trail heading west and follow signs to Snota. The trail starts to climb more steeply, and after an additional two kilometers, passes another intersection with a trail heading north. Stay on the westbound trail, which will turn towards the south and begin a very steep climb up the side of the summit.

The trail here can have snowfields late into the summer, and there are sections that have been a glacier. In the past ten years, the glacier has melted so much that it can sometimes create very slippery and unsafe conditions, and the trail has been rerouted slightly. Follow the trail markings carefully and keep an eye on snow conditions.

Eventually, the trail turns towards the south and then goes up to the summit, here there is a fantastic view over all of Trollheimen.

My notes

I actually didn't make it all the way to the top because I wasn't mentally prepared for the scramble and the slippery sections - I ended up turning around about 150 meters of elevation below the summit. Surprisingly, there is phone service on the mountain, but not in the valley on the way. I recommend taking a light bag and leaving what you don't need at Trollheimshytta - it's a full day hike even with a lighter bag.

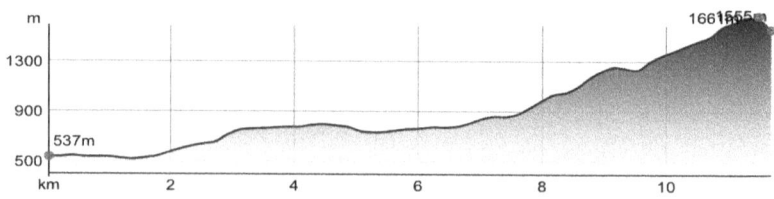

Trollheimshytta to Kårvatn

23.0 km
14.3 miles

559 meters
1,834 feet

886 meters
2,907 feet

8 hours
Challenging

This is a spectacular hike, and while it's long, it's not technically difficult. The trail leaves Trollheimshytta and crosses through a short section of myr, over two bridges. After the trail crosses the second bridge, it climbs up through a birch forest and then goes in between alternating sections of forest and myr, a Norwegian bog. The trail climbs up into the first bowl, where views open up on every side, and then continues to climb through the bowl.

The route goes by a couple of small lakes, then climbs up in between two mountains. There's an emergency shelter close to the midpoint of the path, called Nauståbua. From here, the trail continues along the lake and then the river coming from the lake. There's a section here where the actual path doesn't match what's on UT - follow the marked trail rather than UT, since the marked trail will go up to a new bridge over an impressive gorge.

The last part of the day is sharply downhill through a forest near a waterfall, eventually ending on a forest road that takes you to Kårvatn.

<u>My hiking notes</u>

I absolutely loved this hike - it was one of my first good weather days in Trollheimen, and you have views in all directions. There are plenty of spots to fill up a water bottle and take breaks for snacks.

Nauståbua, the emergency shelter in the middle of the hike, isn't usable for overnight stays. DNT Trondheim has considered building a self-service cabin here to make the day more manageable, but that hasn't happened yet.

Kårvatn is a very fancy self-service cabin, complete with showers and electricity. It's located in a collection of farm buildings, so make sure you have the right building - there's a T on the front and a DNT flag on the building. Prices in the provision room at Kårvatn are slightly higher than other cabins.

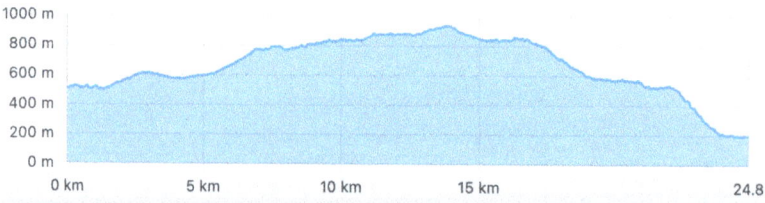

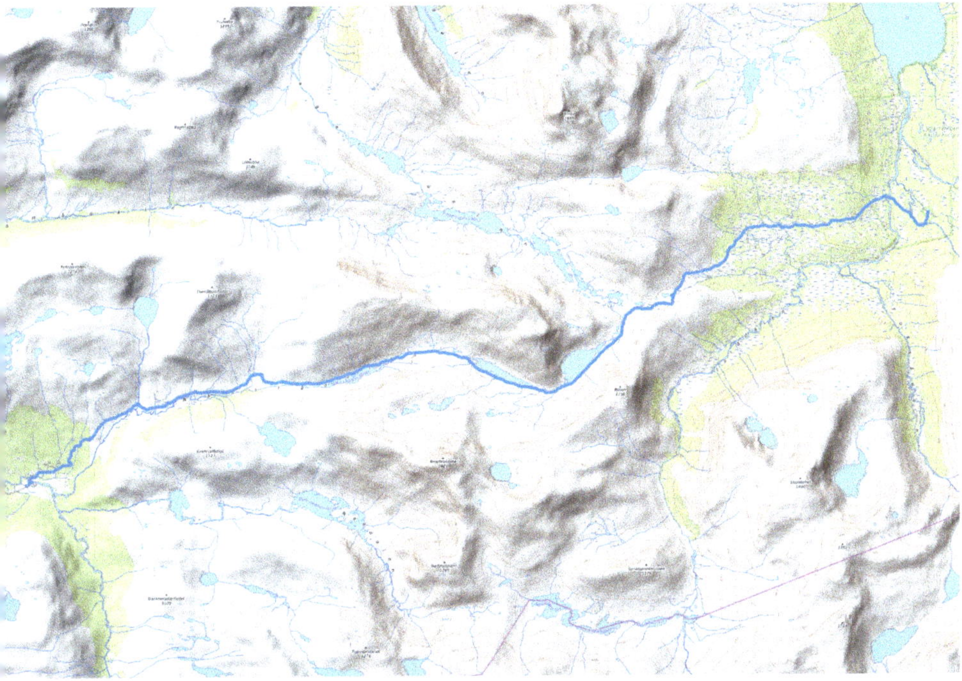

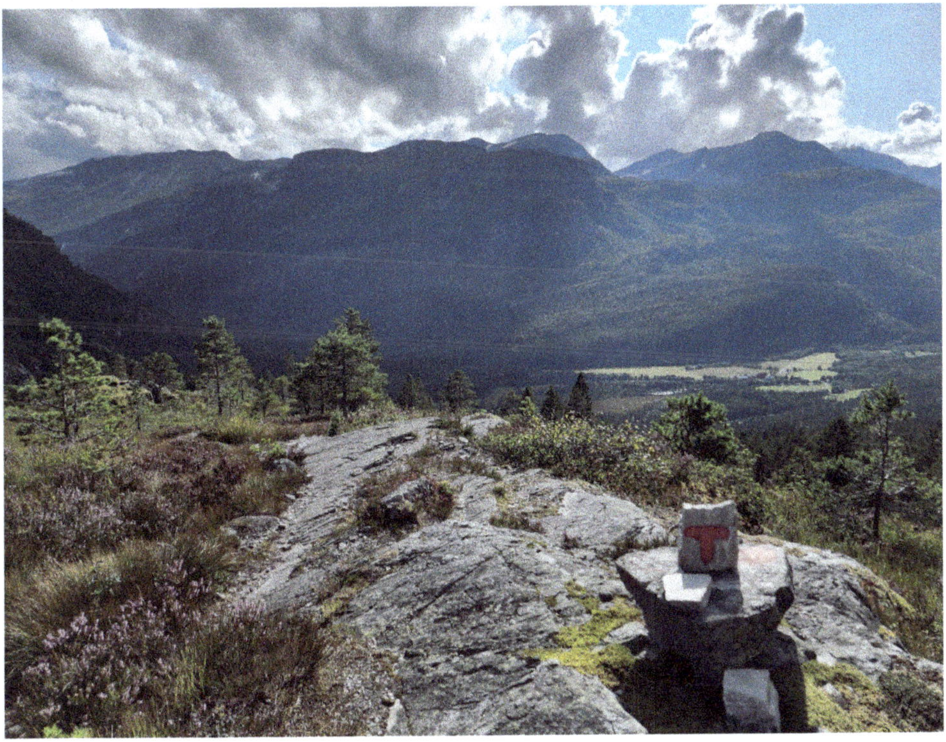

Kårvatn to Innerdalen via Bjøråskaret

| 13.0 km | 978 meters | 781 meters | 5 hours |
| 8.1 miles | 3,209 feet | 2,526 feet | Challenging |

The climb starts on a gravel road that goes out to the trailhead - it's hard to miss it, because there's a large red sign that says "Til Innerdalen". Turn to the left, then follow that trail up through a forest, then through some low shrubs, and eventually into high mountain terrain. Turn around for the views - you can see the fjord in the distance to your right, and waterfalls in the mountains behind you. Eventually, the terrain will start to become rockier. The trail passes the intersection with the path from Todalshytta, then passes a sign marking the halfway point.

The trail climbs until it reaches a lake, Bjøråvatnet at 977 meters above sea level. From here, there's just 200 meters of elevation left until Bjøråskaret. This section is much rockier, and there's a little bit of scrambling. After the saddle, it's just a couple of kilometers down into the Innerdalen, but the trail drops nearly 800 meters of elevation in the course of those few kilometers.

Eventually, the trail reaches the valley and goes through a birch forest, passing some lovely small waterfalls before meeting a tractor road. Turn left to reach Innerdalshytta or right to reach Renndølsetra. If you're lucky, the goats will be out on the road waiting to say hi.

It's also possible to do this hike from Todalshytta. The overall distance is three kilometers shorter, and the trail from Todalshytta climbs up through a forest and the valley until it reaches the path coming from Kårvatn.

My notes

There are two cabin options here, either Renndølsetra or Innerdalshytta. Renndølsetra is private but uses the DNT pricing. When I stayed here, I was the only person at Innerdalshytta, but I've heard from other hikers that it's usually packed.

If you're doing this route in the late summer, there are lots of wild berries along the route that you can pick if you need a hiking snack.

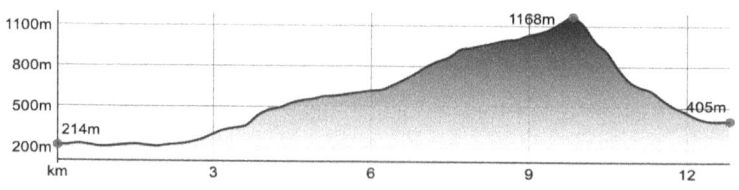

Innerdalen to Bårdsgarden

		↗	↘	🕐
Langvatnet	23.7 km 14.7 miles	891 meters 2,943 feet	670 meters 2,198 feet	8 hours Challenging
Innerdalsporten	22.1 km 13.7 miles	707 meters 2,320 feet	480 meters 1,575 feet	7 hours Challenging

The route over Langvatnet: in total, this is 23.7km and 8 hours of hiking. The path starts on the tractor path in front of Innerdalshytta. Don't cross the river - the path is on the south side, the Innerdalshytta side, of the river and is not the same path as the one coming down from Bjøråskaret. It's a steep climb up alongside the river, gaining elevation quickly. Once you pass the tree line, you'll walk through a bowl next to a lake.

After this bowl, there's another hundred meters of elevation climb out of the bowl to meet Langvatnet on a rocky trail. When the trail starts to go along Langvatnet, the trail is mostly dirt, with some sections with rocks. At the end of the lake, the route starts to go through an open mountain section on dirt trails. The trail over Langvatnet and via Innerdalsporten merge here, approximately 12 kilometers into the hike.

The route via Innerdalsporten: it's 22.1km and 7 hours. Go southwest from Innerdalshytta, then start the route on the north side of a river, going through a birch forest with parts of myr. The trail climbs up towards Innerdalsporten, and continues to gain elevation for three kilometers before meeting the path from Langvatnet.

From where the trails merge, slowly drop elevation going through the open mountain area. The path drops down to run along the side of a lake, Tovatna. As you pass by the lake, it can be wet in parts, although there were planks set out for much of the hike to make it easier. After the lake, the trail goes through gently rolling hills with myr and some small trees. After that, you still have 3km to go on the road until you reach the cabin.

If you don't want to walk to the cabin, you can call and rent a bike when you reach the side of the road. There's a sign in Norwegian with the number to call, and you can pay for the bike with the Hyttebetaling app.

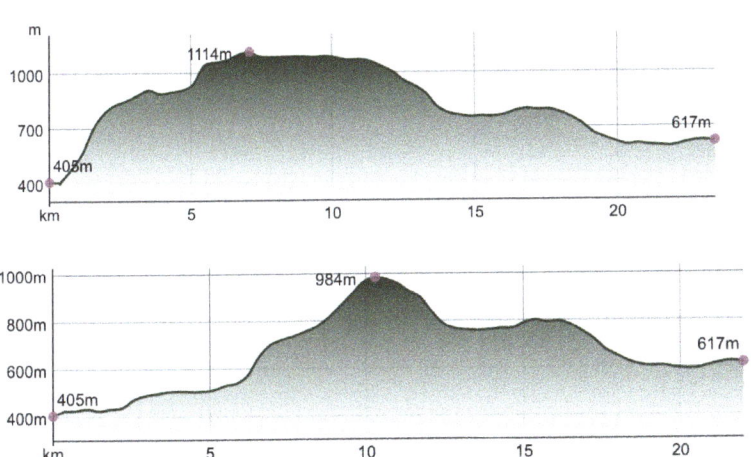

I found that every section of this hike felt longer than I expected from the map. I should have better prepared myself mentally and taken the day more slowly. It's spectacular but can be slow going. If it's been wet, I recommend going over Langvatnet rather than Innerdalsporten to avoid the myr at the beginning of the trail. The trails are similar in difficulty.

Bårdsgarden via Okla to Vassendsetra

18.9 km
11.7 miles

↗

966 meters
3,169 feet

↘

921 meters
3,022 feet

6 hours
Challenging

The trail starts behind Bårdsgarden and climbs through a forest until the turnoff to Okla at three to four kilometers of hiking. The trail climbs up an open area with views onto Okla and the surrounding area. From there, the trail flattens out for a little bit, continuing to be mostly dirt.

Eventually, the trail reaches a rockier section. Follow signs and keep gradually climbing until the viewpoint. This section is difficult because of the amount of rocks underfoot, but it's not steep at all. If you have good views, you'll be able to see out over the lake and towards the rest of Trollheimen.

To reach Vassendsetra from here, turn around and go back to the turnoff at the bottom of the mountain. Turn north at the intersection, following the signs to Vassendsetra for three kilometers until you reach the cabin. The trail goes through a section of forests and myr and is largely flat.

Another option is to continue along the Okla trail rather than turning around, eventually going to Langodden and then walking back along the Gjevilvatnet. That trail is not T-marked or maintained by DNT.

My hiking notes

I definitely recommend Okla - it was spectacular. The view from the top of Okla is so iconic that it was used in chocolate advertising for many years. This was probably my favorite hike of all of Trollheimen - I would add more distance and go along the Gjevilvatnet if I did it again.

Note that some online trail descriptions mention a boat to Gjevilvasshytta - that boat is no longer running.

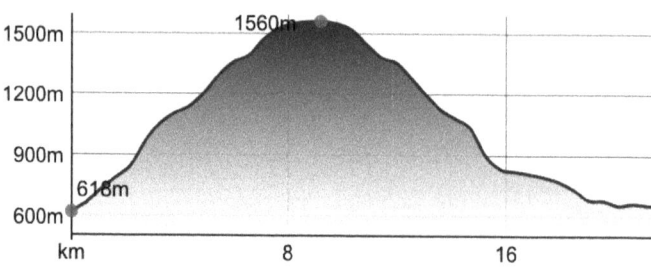

Vassendsetra to Gjevilvasshytta

	👢	↗	↘	🕐
Lake	12.9 km 8.0 miles	194 meters 636 feet	183 meters 600 feet	3.5 hours Moderate
Riaren	22.1 km 13.7 miles	1,005 meters 3,297 feet	994 meters 3,261 feet	7 hours Challenging

There are two options for this section:

Option A: Along the lake

The first option is walking back to Gjevilvasshytta along the lake. The trail hugs the lake and is easy to follow This is an easy hike - approximately 15km and flat. The path can be wet and swampy if it's been raining. The last few kilometers of this hike are on the road to Gjevilvasshytta and are even paved.

Option B: Up and over Riaren

The second option is going up and over Riaren. Start by going west from Vassendsetra, first in myr and then climbing up to an intersection with the trail from Bårdsgarden and the trail to Trollheimshytta at about three kilometers in. From here, follow the signs towards Gjevilvasshytta and Riaren. The trail begins to steeply climb up, heading back towards the east. The trail starts to run along the south side of a lake after an additional three kilometers. This section can have snowfields or very rocky terrain.

Continue along the lake until the trail reaches another intersection with the trail coming from Trollheimshytta. Turn towards the southeast here and follow signs to Gjevilvasshytta. The route climbs up and over Riaren, then turns towards the southeast and begins to gently drop, first through rocky terrain and then through easy, dirt terrain. The trail ends on paved roads as it gets close to Gjevilvasshytta.

My notes

If you have the time for a full day hike, I recommend going up and over Riaren rather than along the lake. There aren't many views from the lake route since it's in a forest most of the time. If you're tired from previous hikes, though, the river is a good way to have a bit of a recovery day.

Blåhøa from Gjevilvasshytta

25.0 km
15.5 miles

1,193 meters
3,914 feet

1,193 meters
3,914 feet

6 hours
Challenging

Start by going along the road from Gjevilvasshytta for 1.5 kilometers, then turn off onto the path towards Trollheimshytta. Check signs and the map through this section - there are several other trails, both summer trails and ski trails, that are marked in the area. I went the wrong way for a little bit.

The trail climbs gently through a large, open section, then crosses over a bridge and continues to walk towards the base of Blåhøa. The climb here is slightly steeper. At the bottom of the mountain next to a lake, the trail to the summit cuts off towards the east. From here, it's a steep climb up Blåhøa in rocky terrain. After climbing up nearly 500 meters in elevation, the trail reaches the summit. The route is well-marked and easy to follow, although the terrain is rocky.

To get back to Gjevilvasshytta, turn around and go back the way you came.

This little spur is from me going the wrong way. Make sure to not get onto the wrong trail in the area near Gjevilvasshytta.

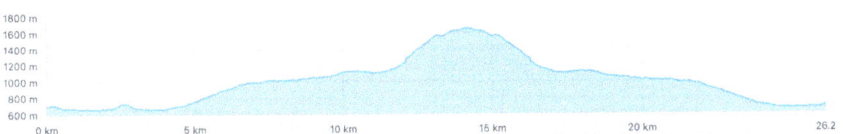

I can't vouch for the views, since I managed to do this hike in a cloud. The people I spoke to at Gjevilvasshytta had great pictures, though. It's quite steep towards the top, but if it's nice weather, there are great places to stop and enjoy the view along the top.

Trollheimshytta to Gjevilvasshytta

21.1 km 13.1 miles	1,027 meters 3,369 feet	853 meters 2,799 feet	8 hours Challenging

The trail starts by crossing over the Slettåa river behind Trollheimshytta. From here, the path runs along the river and then begins to climb steeply up towards Mellomfjellet ("the in between mountain" – as I have mentioned before, the Norwegians love their creative place names). Continue along the top of Mellomfjellet. The trail reaches Fossådalsvatnet at between seven and eight kilometers of hiking, then goes alongside the east side of the lake and continues south another three kilometers until it reaches the intersection with the trail to Blåhøa.

From here, the trail starts to drop elevation, going down through open terrain until it reaches the road to Gjevilvasshytta. The last 1.5 kilometers of the day are on paved roads.

My notes

This is a great hike because it shows so many different Norwegian landscapes - from the high mountains to agricultural lands to lakes. It's almost a Trollheimen in miniature. That being said, it's a long hike and the toughest day on the Trollheimen Triangle.

The second half of the hike is the same as the hike from Vassendsetra to Gjevilvasshytta over Riaren, or as the return from Snota to Gjevilvasshytta.

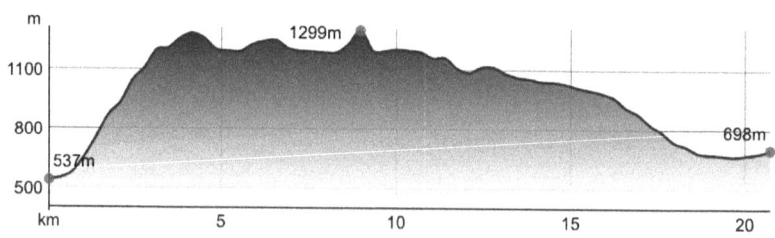

Øvre Sæter to Sætersetra to Vindølbu

| 12.1 km | 958 meters | 545 meters | 4.5 hours |
| 7.5 miles | 3,143 feet | 1,788 feet | Challenging |

Vindølbu is the most southern of the cabins that connect the Fjordruta near Kristiansund to the Trollheimen hiking routes. It's also a good access point from which to start cabin to cabin hikes in Trollheimen. To get to the trailhead, take the 905 bus from Trondheim or Sunndalsora to Øvre Sæter.

From Øvre Sæter, start by climbing up through a forest to Sætersetra, a self-service cabin where you can spend the night or stop and have a snack. From here, climb steeply up to the Grytvatnet (Gryt lake) and then go around the lake towards the east. From here, turn towards the south and then hike along the side of the valley looking out over the Vindalen (Vin valley). This section can be very wet and swampy if there's been a lot of rain.

My notes

Due to construction, there's a temporary route to Sætersetra through at least the end of 2024. It's not marked on UT, and I found it quite difficult to follow. Check UT before you go, or email KNT (the Kristiansund branch of DNT) at turist@knt.no for updates.

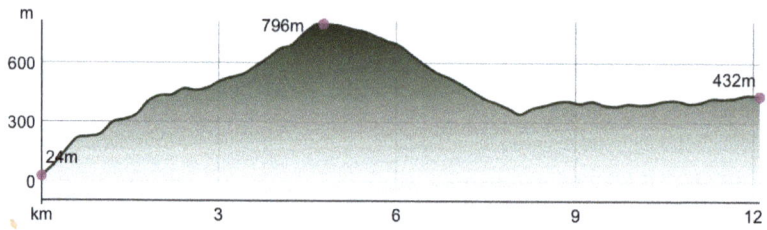

Vindølbu is one of my favorite self-service cabins. It has power and running water, as well as a toilet that doesn't require going outside to reach. Super cozy and a great spot for a rest day.

Vindølbu to Trollheimshytta

| 19.1 km 11.9 miles | 736 meters 2,415 feet | 682 meters 2,238 feet | 6 hours Challenging |

If it's dry, today is largely smooth. There's a short climb up from Vindølbu to the path towards Trollheimshytta, or you can take a lower route that goes by one of the largest trees in Norway. From there, the path goes through fields of myr with mountains on either side. Walk along the north side of the Svartvatnet until the trail reaches an intersection with the trail to Snota. Take the more eastern path and continue towards Trollheimshytta. The path starts to gently drop elevation, heading towards Trollheimshytta. The trail eventually enters a forest and then drops steeply to Trollheimshytta, crossing over a bridge and then through the camping area to reach the cabin.

My notes

This was not a good hike for me. I did it in very heavy rain, and many of the sticks that are used to mark the trail had fallen over. Even after the rain stopped, the fog was too heavy to see the next marker. I ended up fording several rivers that weren't even marked on the map. It was the one hike I've done in Norway so far where I've needed to rely on map and compass - my fingers were too wet to open my phone screen.

1000m
800m
600m
400m
951m
537m
432m
km
4
8
12
16

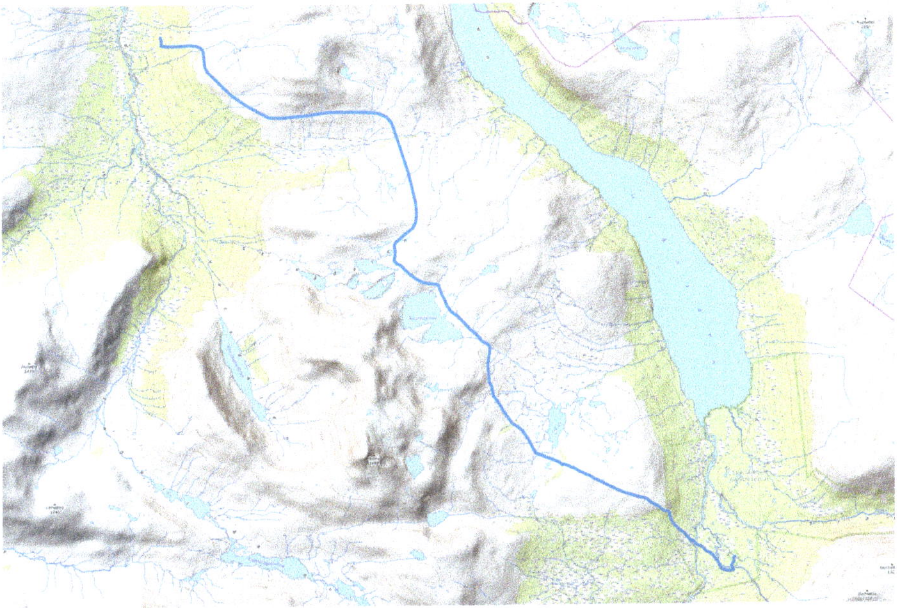

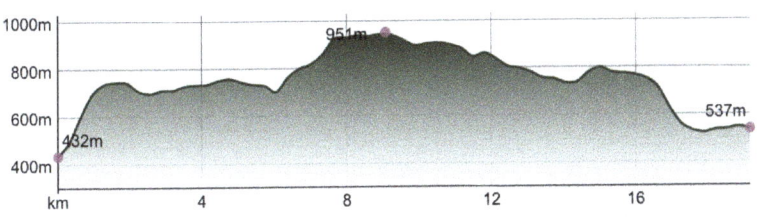

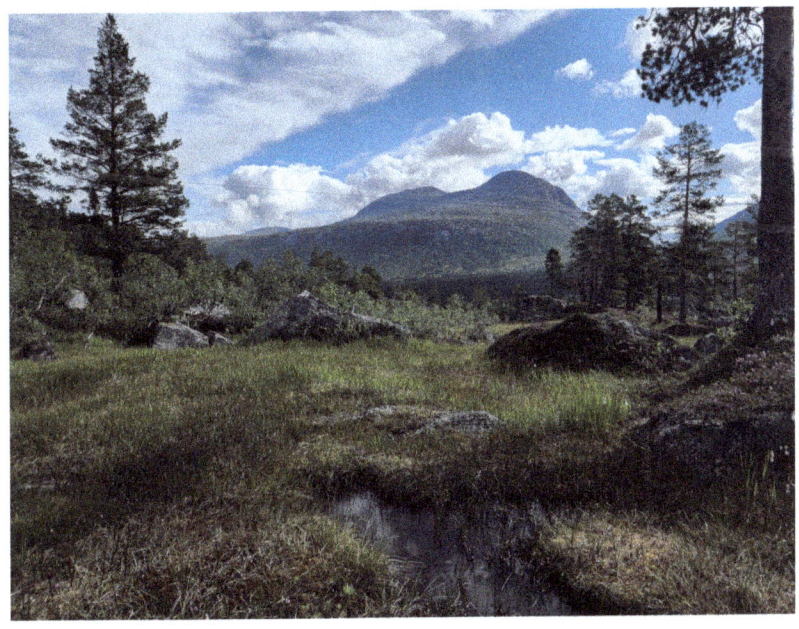

Innerdalshytta to Eiriksvollen

| 14.3 km | 646 meters | 958 meters | 6 hours |
| 8.9 miles | 2,119 feet | 3,143 feet | Challenging |

From Innerdalshytta, the trail crosses over the river Ulvåa, then goes south through a forest along the east side of the Fluo river. Continue along the east side of Storvatnet ("the big lake"). The route continues along the river coming from Storvatnet, then turns towards the east and then drops down to Eiriksvollen.

My notes

Eiriksvollen is located about a ten minute walk to a bus stop, so this is a potential route out of Trollheimen. It also connects into the trail network in Sunndal and Dovrefjell if you want to extend your hike going south.

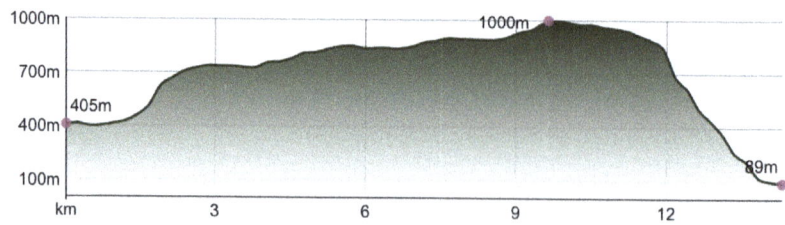

Bårdsgarden to Kårvatn

| 22.0 km | 486 meters | 891 meters | 6 hours |
| 13.7 miles | 1,594 feet | 2,923 feet | Challenging |

The route starts by going along the road to Storlia, where there's a parking lot. After that, the goes along a closed, dirt road and then meets the trail. The trail climbs up along the river to Lontjønna.

From here, the route goes towards the west, eventually running along the north edge of a lake. From here, the trail turns towards the north and then drops through a valley down to Kårvatn, running along the eastern side of a river until reaching a bridge just before Kårvatn.

The valley can be wet if it's rained recently, and there are a few spots with myr. I recommend poles for the descent down to Kårvatn, since it can be quite steep in parts.

My notes

This hike essentially goes in between two of the nicest self-service cabins that you could stay at - both have power and showers. Bårdsgarden even has running water.

If you're driving in, you can park your car at Storlia and cut off some of the morning walk along the road.

My pro tip is to pick up fresh cheese at bread at the farm store at Bårdsgarden and enjoy it along the hike.

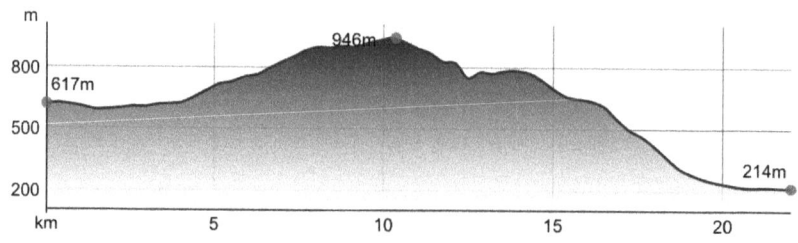

Logistics

Getting There and Back

Only a few of the cabins in Trollheimen are accessible via public transit. To get to those:

- Eiriksvollen: take the 901 bus from Kristiansund or Oppdal to Fale bru. The bus stop is a 5-10 minute walk from the cabin. Five to seven buses a day.

- Gjevilvasshytta: to get to and from Gjevilvasshytta, there are buses to the cabin from the Oppdal train station from July 1 to August 31st, with times coordinated with the train from Oslo. If the bus isn't running, you can also take a taxi from Oppdal, which works out to about 500 NOK. There's an app you can use to call the taxi, called Tronder Taxi, or you can call the taxi service directly – the taxi drivers speak perfect English.

- Sætersetra and Vindølbu: take the 905 bus from Trondheim or Sunndalsora to Øvre Sæter, then hike in. The bus runs 2-3 times a day.

If you have your own car, you can also drive to Bårdsgarden, Kårvatn, Innerdalshytta, or Todalshytta. There's parking a 2 hour walk from Jøldalshytta as well.

Timing

The snow melts fairly early in Trollheimen, so it's possible to start hiking in late June. Check SeNorge.no for the latest on the snow cover and conditions. The trails usually stay snow free into late September, although the cabins will start closing their serviced portions in early September.

Many of the cabins are also open for ski season, although the trails are not groomed. If you want to go during the winter, you'll need to be familiar with backcountry/cross-country skiing ("fjellski") in the Norwegian mountains.

Supplies

There are very few places to restock on supplies other than the cabins. There's a shop at Kårvatn with limited opening hours and a cafe at Bårdsgarden. Otherwise, the self-service cabins in Trollheim are generally well-stocked.

I recommend bringing some additional lunch supplies and some fresh food with you for the self-service cabins. I generally like to bring parmesan cheese and pesto for pasta, as well as cheese and sandwich toppings for lunches. There is always enough to eat in the cabins, but it's not always delicious.

Camping

Norway has some of the most permissive laws in the world around camping. Norway has a law called the Allemannsretten that guarantees the ability of people to explore and experience nature, even in privately owned areas, as long as you're in uncultivated land. Once you're in the wilderness, you may camp in any area, as long as you're at least 150 meters away from the nearest inhabited house or cabin.

Note that the 150 meters applies to the DNT cabins as well - most cabins have marked areas where you can camp, and you'll have to pay a small fee to use the toilets or other common facilities. Trollheimshytta and Kårvatn both had designated camping areas when I went.

Campfires are prohibited everywhere in Norway from April 15 to September 15. You will need to bring a gas stove to cook, and in the case of drought, even gas stoves may be banned.

Trollheimen is a great place to camp - the terrain tends not to be rocky, so there are plenty of spots to put up a tent. The only thing to note is that camping can be limited around Innerdalshytta, Kårvatn, or Bårdsgarden, where there are active farms. You may also want to camp a couple kilometers away from the cabins to avoid sheep coming to visit.

Planning Resources

yr.no is the best resource for weather in Norway. It allows you to hike by specific cabin or mountaintop, with the weather for that particular point rather than the overall area. It's available in English.

Senorge.no shows the current and historic weather conditions for any point in Norway. It's very useful for checking the amount of snow remaining for summer hikes, as well as seeing if it's rained recently.

ut.no is unfortunately only in Norwegian, but is the best source of information on cabins and trails. You can download offline maps by going to "Profil" and then "Mine offline-kart" on the app, and the website is great for seeing trails at a high level.

Varsom.no is key for the winter and shows storm and avalanche warnings. It's available in English.

enTUR.no is the best source for public transportation information. Google Maps's public transit is not reliable in Norway.

If you're stopping by a DNT office before going hiking, you can pick up a planleggingskart, or planning map. These aren't usable for hiking but are great for planning, since they show the locations of cabins and DNT cabins.

Fjellvettreglene (Norwegian Mountain Code)

The Norwegian Mountain Code contains the guidelines for having a safe trip in the Norwegian mountains. They're considered an important part of Norwegian cultural heritage and were introduced after a spate of fatal accidents in 1950.

1. Plan your trip and inform others about the route you have selected.

2. Adapt the planned routes according to ability and conditions.

3. Pay attention to the weather and the avalanche warnings.

4. Be prepared for bad weather and frost, even on short trips.

5. Bring the necessary equipment so you can help yourself and others.

6. Choose safe routes. Recognize avalanche terrain and unsafe ice.

7. Use a map and a compass. Always know where you are.

8. Don't be ashamed to turn around

9. Conserve your energy and seek shelter if necessary.

In case of emergency, notify the police at 112. You can also call 911 or 999, and the dispatch will connect you to the correct service. Within the cabins, there are signs giving the coordinates of the cabins and the emergency numbers.

Packing List

In total, the gear below should weigh between 15 and 25 pounds (7 to 12 kilograms).

Gear

☐ 46-55 liter hiking backpack with a rain shield

☐ Maps and compass: *the maps in this guide are overview maps, and I strongly recommend getting 1:50,000 hiking maps just in case you're caught out in low visibility conditions or your phone battery dies (see: my experience between Vindølbu and Trollheimshytta).*

☐ Hiking poles: *I used them to poke the ground to make sure it was real ground and not just mud, and to take the pressure off my knees on downhills*

☐ Duct tape

☐ Dry bags for packing

☐ First aid kit

Clothing

☐ Hiking boots

☐ Rain pants and optional gaiters: *in myr or grasses, the water from plants nearby will soak into your pants if you don't have rain pants or gaiters.*

☐ Rain jacket

☐ Windbreaker: *it's frequently misting in the mornings, so if you don't like hiking in your rain jacket, bring a lighter weight jacket to hike in*

☐ Wool socks, two pairs: *I use one pair of socks for hiking and one pair for the cabin.*

☐ Hiking pants or long underwear to layer under rain pants

☐ Two sports bras and two pairs of underwear

☐ Wool sweater

☐ Extra warm jacket

☐ Hat and gloves

☐ Two hiking shirts

Things I've learned the hard way: make sure your rain gear and shoes are still waterproof *before* you start the hike. And bring dry bags for inside your backpack.

Cabin Supplies

☐ Mini towel: *for cabins with showers. The showers are usually single gender but communal, so the towel is handy even if you want to create a little shield to get changed under.*

☐ DNT key

☐ Sengetøy (sheet set) or sleep liner: *required for the cabins*

☐ Toilet shoes: *about half of the cabins have outdoor toilet, and this keeps you from having to put potentially wet hiking boots back on*

☐ Sleep mask: *there are good curtains in the cabins, but it never gets dark*

Food and Drink

☐ Thermos for hot drinks

☐ Small plastic water bottle: *there are plenty of spots to refill along the way on every day of the hike, and I found it easier to have a small bottle I could fill up and drink than a hydration system*

☐ Candy and snacks

☐ Plastic bag for sandwiches

Tech

☐ Phone: *I recommend downloading UT, YR, and Hyttebetaling before your hike*

☐ Battery pack: *the cabins except Vassendsetra have power, but just in case*

☐ Chargers: *many of the cabins only have USB classic charging outlets. If you have a phone with a USB-C charging port, you will want to bring a USB to USB-C charger.*

Other

☐ ID and credit cards: *all of the cabins are payable with the Hyttebetaling app, so there's no need to bring cash*

☐ Sunglasses and sunscreen: *almost the entire hike is unshaded, so if it's sunny, you'll need sunscreen*

☐ Toiletries - wilderness wash, face wash, toothpaste, toothbrush, contacts, contact lens solution, glasses, hairbrush, hair ties, nail clippers, any medications you take as needed

☐ Tiny shovel and toilet paper

☐ Extra plastic bags

Some Handy Norwegian Words

Almost all Norwegians speak perfect English. That said, there are times where it's handy to be able to read signs, the weather, or the map.

Hiking and the map

Bratt/meget bratt: steep/very steep

Breen: the glacier

Dalen: the valley

Grusvei: a gravel path

Luftig: steep drop offs on the side of the trail

Kvistet: marked (used for ski trails)

Merket: marked (used for summer trails)

Mobildekning: phone service

Myr: a swampy, wet land covering

Nord, sor, ost, vest: north, south, east, west

Skog: forest

Stein: rocky

Steinur: rocky patches to hike over

Tind/tinden: peak

Vadested: a place that requires wading

Vannet: the water

Varder: cairns

Vatnet: the lake

Vegen: road

Weather

Bris: breeze

Flom: flood

Lettskyet: barely cloudy

Lyn: lighting

Nedbør: precipitation

Nysnø: new snow (no icy cover yet)

Regn: rain

Weather continued

Skyet: cloudy

Snø: snow

Sol: sun

Soloppgang, solnedgang: sunrise, sunset

Strynregen: very heavy rain

Tåkete: foggy

Torden: thunder

Things in provision rooms

Bønnemix: mixed beans

Erter: peas

Fullkorn: whole grain

Gryte: stew

Hermetikk: shelf-stable boxes

Kaffe: coffee

Kanel: cinnamon

Kokemalt: coffee that needs to be cooked in a kettle

Kjeks: biscuits

Kjøtt: meat

Knekkebrød: crispbread

Kokk uten lokk: cook without a lid

Kylling: chicken

Lapskaus: a Norwegian stew of potatoes and meat

Legg til: add to (e.g. "legg til vann" = "add water")

Linser: lentils

Melkepulver: milk powder (reconstitute with water)

Ost: cheese

Pannekake: pancakes

Food continued

Potetmos: mashed potatoes

Rein: reindeer

Ror godt: stir well

Smør: butter

Sodd: a high calorie stew of pork, potatoes, and some vegetables

Sukker: sugar

Svine: pork

Syltetøy: jam

Turmat: dehydrated hiking food

Vann: water

Cabins

Betjent: serviced (a lodge)

Selvbetjent: self-service (a cabin without staff but with a provision room)

Ubetjent: unserviced (a cabin with beds, propane, and wood, but no food)

Drikkevann: drinking water

Forhåndsbestilt: booked in advance

Hyttefelt: a collection of cabins

Protokoll: the book you have to sign when you arrive at a cabin

Sikringshytta: a smaller, secondary cabin next to a main cabin ("hovedhytta")

Using the Cabins

One of the most amazing things about hiking in Norway is the national cabin network. The Norwegian Trekking Association (DNT) maintains a network of more than 600 cabins spread across the country. It makes it easy to travel deep into the wilderness without carrying food or a tent.

Cabins come in three grades:

Betjent (serviced):

These aren't cabins but full lodges. You'll have a three course meal for dinner, a buffet breakfast with a place to fill your thermos, showers and drying rooms for clothes, and often indoor toilets.

Dinners are served family style, where the staff will bring out giant tureens of soup for a first course, then usually some kind of meat and potatoes, then individual desserts. There's more than enough food for everyone - but make sure to book ahead and alert the cabin if you're vegetarian or have dietary restrictions.

The family style dinners mean that you have to go to an assigned dinner time, usually seven o'clock, rather than eating whenever. There's usually assigned seating as well, which means that you'll be put with other travelers. People are generally very friendly and strike up conversations.

You'll pack lunch for the next day at breakfast. There is parchment paper and sometimes plastic bags for taking sandwiches in - the Norwegians are generally happy to show you how to wrap a sandwich in parchment paper if you need help. The stay at a serviced cabin also includes a thermos fill up for the next morning - they'll let you know at check in if you fill it up yourself or leave your thermos at the reception desk the night before.

Serviced cabins have electricity but a limited number of outlets for charging devices. Outlets are often only in the common areas and not in the sleeping rooms. Serviced cabins also have drying rooms and showers. Drying rooms usually have strong heaters and dehumidifiers that dry out gear overnight.

Selvbetjent (self-service)

Self-service cabins are unique to Norway. They're generally smaller than staffed cabins, but come fully stocked with a provisions room, wood for the fireplace, gas for cooking, and cooking supplies like pots and pans. Some have electricity, but it's usually from a single solar panel and is only enough to charge one or two phones. You usually have to fetch and boil water from a nearby water source.

The self-service and unserviced cabins run on the honor system. You'll have to use your DNT key to lock and unlock the cabins - you can purchase the key at a physical DNT store in Norway, online at their web store, or at a staffed cabin. To pay for your stay, use the Hyttebetaling app. The app allows you to keep a list of all the supplies you've used and then pay with credit card when you get back into phone service. The app is available in English.

Ubetjent (unserviced)

These are just like self-service cabins, except that there isn't food available in the provision room. Some of the serviced cabins in Trollheimen are unserviced during the low season.

Cabin Etiquette:

When you arrive at an unserviced or self-service cabin, the first thing to do is to unlock the cabin and then take off your shoes. No outdoor shoes are allowed in the cabin to help keep it clean. After that, fill in your information in the besøksprotokoll, a horizontal blue book that asks where you came from, where you're going, and your membership information. After that, you have the right to use the cabin. I generally first start a fire if the cabin is cold, then fetch water to heat up for dinner.

When you leave the cabin in the morning, you'll need to clean up. That means washing all of the dishes, cleaning out the ashes in the fireplace, bringing in fresh wood for the fire, washing the floors in the bedroom and common areas, and any other tidying.

You can use the cabins if you're camping. You'll need to register in the besøksprotokoll and pay for a day visit ("dagsbesøk"). After that, you can cook food or just relax for a bit. Make sure to sweep up and wash the floors after yourself.

Cabin FAQs:

It's not necessary to book in advance for any of the cabins - if you arrive at the cabin, you'll have a place to sleep, though it might be on a mattress on the floor if it's really busy. I generally don't book cabins in advance so that I have the most flexibility possible to change hiking plans based on the weather.

The exception to this rule is if you have dietary restrictions. Because meals at serviced cabins are served family style, the cabins need advance notice to be able to accommodate these.

Joining DNT:

If you're using the cabins, you should absolutely join DNT - the savings on staying in the cabin will cover the cost of the membership in two to three nights. Non-members pay 15% extra on everything, including stay and cost of food.

If you are planning to camp, you will likely still want to join DNT to get a DNT key. You'll need the key if you want to do a day visit or if you end up staying in a cabin during a day with particularly bad weather. The only cabin in Trollheimen that is usually locked is Vassendsetra, but that can change.

Joining online is a little confusing, and there are updated instructions on the blog. You can also stop by any DNT office in Norway.

Cooking at the cabin:

There is a propane stove and plenty of cooking supplies in the cabins. The food that you'll generally find breaks down into four categories:

Breakfast: knekkebrød, oatmeal mixes, pancake mix, leverposti (liver spread), jam and chocolate spread, mackerel in tomatoes, butter, jam, and honey

Dinner: fish soup, peas and carrots, mashed potato mix, lapskaus, rice, bacalo, boxed mixes for Pasta di Parma and Chili Con Carne, pasta, reindeer meatballs, dry red lentils, and crushed tomatoes

Snacks and dessert: chocolate pudding, vanilla sauce , canned fruit in syrup, and biscuits

Misc things: dried hiking food, coffee, tea, hot chocolate, currant drink mix, hiking snacks like knekkebrød sandwiches, sugar, cinnamon

Each cabin has a different selection of food, and if you're late in the season, certain items might be eaten up. If you're vegetarian or gluten-free, make sure to have your own backup food.

My challenge with cooking at self-service cabins is finding something to bring for lunch the next day. I really load up on breakfast, often mixing vanilla sauce or jam into my oatmeal for the extra calories. I take two or three packages of freeze dried food with me to eat on the trail, in case there isn't shelf-stable cheese and knekkebrød for lunch.

Cabin Amenities

Cabin	Cabin Type	Total Beds	Bookable	Power
Gjevilvasshytta	Serviced	64	64	Yes, 220 V
Jøldalshytta	Serviced	94	94	Yes, 12 V
Trollheimshytta	Serviced	80	80	Yes, 12 V
Kårvatn	Self-service	18	0	Yes, 220 V
Innerdalshytta	Serviced	81	81	Yes, 220 V
Bårdsgarden	Self-service	20	0	Yes, 220 V
Vassendsetra	Self-service	27	21	N
Renndølsetra	Private serviced	24	24	Yes, 220 V
Sætersetra	Self-service	8	0	N
Vindølbu	Self-service	15	0	Yes, 12 V
Todalshytta	Serviced	27	27	Yes, 220 V
Eiriksvollen	Self-service	14	0	Yes, 12 V

Phone Service	Drying Room	Shower	Other Notes
Y	Y	Y	There's an unserviced cabin without showers or drying room that can be used during off season
N	Y	N	Can borrow boats to go out on the lake here. I had some phone service, but that's not guaranteed
N	Y	Y	
N	N	Y	
Y	Y	Y	Self-service outside of the main hiking season
Y	N	Y	Huge, fancy self-service cabin. There's a farm stand nearby to buy fresh bread and cheese
N	N	N	Locked with the DNT key
Y	Y	Y	Private alternative to Innerdalshytta
Y	N	N	One of DNT's least visited cabins, so the provision room may be sparse
Y	N	N	Unlocked
Y	N	Y	Shorter open season than other serviced cabins; make sure to check before you go. 4 bed self-service quarters when the main cabin is closed
Y	N	N	Access point into Trollheimen

Trollheimen FAQs

Can I drink the water underway? Do I need to bring a water filter?
You can drink water directly from streams in Norwegian national parks, and there are plenty of small streams to fill up at. Around Jøldalshytta and Gjevilvasshytta, though, there are sheep and goats grazing, and you can't drink the water once you're less than 1 or 2 kilometers from the cabin. I went without a water filter and filled up in the sheep free zones.

Can I leave luggage?
If you're flying in, the best place to leave your luggage is at the Oslo or Trondheim airport. Both airports have luggage lockers that you can rent for between $7 and $10/day. Officially, the luggage lockers can only be used for seven days, but there is no problem keeping it there longer. Email hittegods.osl@no.issworld.com (Oslo) or hittegods.trd@wideroe.no (Trondheim) or and let them know your locker number and plans.

There are also luggage lockers at the Oppdal train station rented out by Speed Locker. I was unable to find a staff person to talk to me about time restrictions on those.

Can I go in May or October?
The short answer is maybe, but I wouldn't recommend it. Check SeNorge to see how much snow cover is left in May or has already arrived in October. The snow melt also means that rivers can be very high and hard to cross, and summer bridges are generally not put out until the beginning to middle of June.

Is it expensive?
It's about $100/night to stay in a serviced cabin, which includes all food, and $30/night to stay in a self-service cabin. It's a lot cheaper than other hiking trips I've taken because you don't have to pay for a hotel room - you pay by person rather than room. If you want to save on the cost, you can camp some nights rather than staying in the cabins.

Can I do laundry along the way?
You can hand wash clothes at the serviced cabins and then dry them in the drying room, but that's it. There are no laundry facilities.

Can I rely on the self-service cabins to have food and supplies?
Yes - I've visited 81 DNT cabins so far and have yet to find one that wasn't stocked. If you have dietary restrictions, though, make sure to bring some backup food. There is always food, but it is not always what you're craving.

Are there bugs?
I didn't think so, but it was windy when I went. I might take a small thing of bug spray if bugs like to bite you.

Am I okay just speaking English?
Absolutely. In my entire time in Norway, I have met only three people who couldn't speak English. The only challenge is that the labels on food in the self-service cabins are only in Norwegian. I've included some key words in the book for reading food labels.

How hard is navigation?
Generally it's not too tough - the trails are really well marked, and because Trollheimen is a pretty popular national park, you can usually see the trail on the ground as well. I still recommend bringing maps and a compass just in case.

How is phone service in Trollheimen?
It's mixed - generally it's pretty good, but there are a few sections near Trollheimshytta and Vassendsetra that are dead zones.

What's the biggest mistake people make with this hike?
Going too early in the season and/or assuming it will be warm during the summer. The Norwegian hiking season doesn't begin until late June or early July, and even then, there can be substantial snow left. Be prepared for cold weather and rain, even hiking in July or August. It's rare for the temperature to be above 20 degrees Celsius, even in late summer.

Sarah Rowe has solo hiked more than 3,500 kilometers across 21 countries, with a focus on Norway and Austria. When she's not out in the mountains, she's drinking coffee, writing about hiking on her blog, Solo Female Wanderer, or planning the next adventure. She lives in the northeastern United States, two kilometers from the Appalachian Trail.

Questions or comments? You can reach her at sarah@solofemalewanderer.com.